LIVING AND LOVING WELL

LIVING AND LOVING WELL

A Field Guide

by
Joseph Stuczynski, PMP

First paperback printing January 2008
ISBN: 978-0-6151-9316-8

Published with Lulu

Manufactured and printed in the United States of America

Cover photo by Joseph Stuczynski
For more photos go to: http://www.onefinepixel.com

Preface

IS THIS BOOK FOR YOU?

"Living and Loving Well" [LLW] *is a specific method that heightens your awareness of both your Core Values and the qualities you desire in relationships. A strong set of core values governs your future actions and decisions, as well as the people and situations you attract. When not given the opportunity to develop these self-affirming items, you adopt your parents' (or care givers') behaviors and decision-making skills, which often times create self-doubt and inner conflict in many areas of your life. This confusion is based on the limited understanding we have of ourselves, the relationships we want or the people we want to attract.*

The LLW method affirms the reality that your life can be lived on your own terms. Living a well-defined life means attracting friends, colleagues or romantic partners that are aligned with your Core Values. It also means reducing and eventually eliminating the amount of times you find yourself in unfulfilling or unhealthy situations.

LLW is different from other self-improvement books because:

- *It's designed around your Core Values. As mentioned above when you're not given the opportunity to create them, you adopt your parent's behaviors and decision-making skills, which are commonly referred to as patterns. These produce the anxiety and frustration you feel when continuing to find Mr/Miss Wrong or making the same mistakes even though you know better. Creating a set of beliefs or values is the first step to breaking patterns and living a life DEFINED by YOU.*

- *It adopts similar methods used by successful companies that design and communicate values and Mission Statements to create a clear and unified direction, as well as to help employees make better decisions. We as individuals should have the same opportunities.*

- *It's written as a field guide to accommodate the demands of a hectic lifestyle, and intended to provide only the necessary information and exercises that will produce the maximum results in your life.*

- *It goes beyond the general explanation of why we repeat patterns in our relationships, and through the process, **STOPS** them from repeating. **LLW** provides four simple exercises so that your life is based on your spirit and not old habits and patterns, which have a tendency to limit our individual development.*

*Ask yourself the following questions, and if you answer yes to any of them, the **LLW** method will change your life considerably.*

- *Are you single and tired of attracting the same unfulfilling relationships?*
- *Do your relationships feel as if they're missing something?*
- *Do you want to 'fine tune' or identify areas for improvement in your marriage or current relationship?*
- *Are you satisfied with the relationships in your life but want a better understanding of yourself, and the values that guide you?*
- *Do you feel as if your patterns are bigger or more powerful than you?*
- *Have you stopped trusting your decisions when it comes to love, work and other relationships?*
- *Do you keep making the same mistakes even though you feel as if you should have already learned 'that lesson'?*

Acknowledgements

Thanks to my writing group Donna and Jorge. Special thanks to Donna for editing many versions and making thoughtful suggestions, which were always true to the spirit of this project.

Thanks to my family and friends.

To Earl and Beatrice Worthington-Farnsworth.

A very special thanks to Jill Richburg for endless hours of conversation solving the world's problems, and allowing me the space and time to brainstorm new ideas, for being stupid, improvising and being a damn good friend.

And last but certainly not least, to Lawrence Ferrara whose support, dedication and unwavering loyalty acts as a beacon of hope so I always find my way home. He shows me how to live and love well. This book is dedicated to him.

LIVING AND LOVING WELL

A Field Guide

Contents

We are our life's purpose.

We hear that love is blind.

Don't believe it. If love is blind, then we are condemned to live like a piece of driftwood that has no choice about where it goes or about what happens to it.

If I say to myself instead, 'I LOVE WITH CLEAR & FOCUSED INSIGHT', then it becomes possible for me to attract people and situations based on my Core Values, a love that I guide and that in turn fulfills my heart and spirit.

The Mission of Living and Loving Well

To educate and provide techniques that create healthier relationships, better decision-making, increased confidence and life long changes.

To heighten awareness of one's Core Values.

To facilitate the creation of personal life statements.

To help individuals re-define love for themselves.

To expand the overall well being of the human spirit.

Introduction

YOU are unique among billions! You may share similar thoughts about a political topic, you may feel the same about religion and relationships, or your ambitions could be identical to someone living down the street. The one thing that separates you from the other 6.3 billion people on the planet is how you define your place in the world. In other words, the values that guide your decisions and actions, and the relationship qualities you seek (and attract) are absolutely, singularly unique to YOU, and ONLY YOU. The combination of these values and qualities are the foundation to your choices, romance, business situations, friendships and actions. When you define your self with clear intention, the world WILL change because what you tolerate, the relationships you attract, the choices you make, or even how you respond to a situation, changes with it.

It may seem impossible to imagine that changing the way you define yourself, could have such a drastic ripple effect in the world around you, but it's true. It's the same principle found in the Law of Attraction, the Universe will provide based on your will. While I don't know anything about your personal history, I will assume that you have not spent time defining several things: your Core Values, supporting value statements or a full list of qualities that you expect to both give and receive in ALL of the relationships in your life.

"Living and Loving Well" [LLW] is a process that focuses on the development of YOUR unique Core Values (or beliefs). A strong set of personal values will guide all of your future actions and decisions. When not given the opportunity to create them, you adopt your parent's behaviors and decision-making skills, which are commonly referred to as patterns. These produce the anxiety and frustration you feel when 'continuing to find Mr./Miss Wrong' or making the 'same mistakes even though you know better.'

Creating a set of beliefs or values is the first step to breaking patterns and living a life as DEFINED by YOU.

LLW is powerful because it eliminates unhealthy and unfulfilling patterns by raising your personal awareness. Sound simple? It is. If you're like me, you've tried therapy and read self help books but never felt that either actually stopped these patterns from recurring. I guarantee that if you follow the full 4-step method you'll walk away with new insight and improved confidence to attract the people and situations you want.

Let's face it; ALL relationships can be difficult. The majority of us go month-to-month even year-to-year wondering if there's a magic formula to finding the 'right' romance, friendships or work dynamic that fits you. Many of us ask ourselves why we continue to repeat the same unhealthy patterns over and over and over. The repetition can be extremely frustrating especially since as adults we'd like to think our intellect has more control over the direction our lives take.

LLW is an innovative collection of tools and techniques that teach you how to define personal values, supporting statements, as well as how to identify qualities that you desire in all relationships. It can also help those already in relationships 'fine tune' or identify areas for improvement. Sometimes we just don't know ourselves well enough to fix the problem.

LLW is an introspective way of looking at your life; it challenges you to understand why you love the way we do, how you choose the people you love, and is effective for enhancing all relationships, whether in business, in romance or with family and friends.

In regard to relationships, most of us were never taught *how* to love, which means that we were most likely never taught how to relate to other people. Too often we go through life repeating the same relationships we observed in our parents or earliest caregivers. As a result, many of the experiences and people we attract are based on a pattern we observed, and not as defined by our own spirit.

The **LLW** method positively changes the type of people and situations we attract. After using this program your inner spirit acquires the knowledge, inclination and power to create positive experiences. You are greater than the accumulation of your old patterns - both good and bad. We all have the ability to re-educate ourselves so that we can feel confident about the decisions we make.

LLW is designed to be a 'field guide' or 'pocket companion' to cater to the pace of busy people's lives. Each of its four [4] exercises will add value to your life. If you only complete one of the exercises, you will have done something positive for yourself, although doing all of them, of course, will provide the most benefit. All aspects of your life will improve if you commit a few hours to understanding the principles of **Living and Loving Well**. Your whole world will shift positively when you re-align your life by having a clear and thoughtful definition of your values, your dreams, your priorities and your self.

What **LLW** is *not*;

- **LLW** is not a guarantee that your life will change. Your world will only change if you *will* it to change. To quote a very popular book, "Thy *will* be done." Wanting something is a lot different from willing it. To say that you are willing to change implies that you're also willing to accept the responsibility to do the work, and willing to accept the outcome, good or bad. "I want to fall in love" has a much different meaning from, "I am willing to fall in love".

- **LLW** is not a PhD.. thesis or psychotherapy. It *is* a practical guide that provides a few simple, rewarding techniques for improving the world you live in, and for providing solutions to some seemingly unsolvable dilemmas.

- **LLW** is not a guide for finding your 'soul mate' or The One. What is does do is help you 'erase the board' so that you can start from the beginning to identify your values, to make some clear statements about the life you desire and finally to define love for yourself.

This world is a big place with many different options so let's get you closer to knowing how to make really good, long-term satisfying choices, the kind that will lead you into the life you truly want.

While you go through this manual, remember that the goal of this whole process is to maximize your experiences while still on this planet which can be done by living a well-defined life.

Using this field guide

Your life is made up of many different relationships including work, love, family and friends. The common denominator is a strong set of Core Values, which guide all of your decisions and actions from whom you choose to date to the type of work relationships you attract.

Option 1 - Relationships: The full method is designed to identify the best qualities for ALL of your relationships. If you're single it creates a baseline for what you want to attract in the future, and if you're currently in a relationship it will fine-tune areas for improvement. This process also develops your Core Values and Life Statements.

Option 2 – Values & Life Statements: Focus solely on Exercise 2 & 3, which help you create your Core Values and Life Statements. This is the foundation to the relationships exercises, so you'll be prepared if you choose to complete that option at a future date.

Daily Mantra

Repeat each of these four [4] sentences emphasizing the words in bold. While thinking of a specific part of your life, such as relationships or work, say them over and over for five [5] minutes at any time or any place, driving your car or in the shower. The result will be a moment of clarity and ownership of your life.

THIS *is my life!*

This **IS** *my life!*

This is **MY** *life!*

This is my **LIFE***!*

1

How This Got Started

Have you ever asked yourself any of the following questions?

- *Why do I repeat patterns in my relationships?*
- *Why do I keep making the same mistakes?*
- *What is it that my relationship is missing?*
- *Why do my decisions go against my better judgment?*
- *How can I attract people/ situations more aligned with my spirit?*

If so, you'll understand when I share with you that I created this program out of complete desperation. Regardless of what books I read or how many times I changed therapists, I continually found myself attracting the same unfulfilling romantic relationships, friendships and work situations. What was most maddening was that sometimes the situations were extreme caricatures of what I *knew* to be unhealthy. In romance, my behaviors and actions weren't always true to who I felt I was at the time. In friendship, I would attract people who didn't support my goals and dreams, and at work, I commonly found myself in difficult and untrusting situations. A coincidence you say? Well, from an intellectual perspective, I was utterly baffled, and emotionally, I was exhausted. If I knew better why didn't I make better choices?

I was determined to figure out why it seemed I had little input in the people and situations I attracted in my life. It had gotten to a point where I no longer trusted my romantic decisions, I was avoiding some of my friends, and my relationships at work felt strained. For six months, I practically hid from humanity, focusing solely on understanding why my patterns seemed bigger than me.

Over a period of time the following thoughts established the gateway to the elusive '*why*' that I had been searching for all along.

1. I was a pattern junkie. All of the situations and relationships in my life were dependent on habitual, established patterns. Whether or not I was aware of what those specific patterns were, I was addicted to them, unable to choose not to. The patterns ruled all of my relationships. I was not in charge!

2. My family - including my siblings, parents and grandparents - shared variations of the same patterns.

3. In my family, no one was ever taught *how* to love or how to nourish a positive relationship.

4. We don't know what we don't know. I couldn't pinpoint my problem, because I was never taught to recognize it. How can any of us recognize something we can't see? Our grandparents, caregivers, parents and everyone else in our 'family tree' have inherited what they know. Without thinking about it, they pass along to the next generation the dynamics, the attitudes, and the behavioral patterns that they learned and observed from their parents.

5. We *seek and teach* what is known and *recognizable* to us based on our experiences. No one had ever taught me the skills I needed in order to have successful relationships. Human beings are creatures of habit so it's no surprise to think that we subconsciously or chemically attract others who recognize the same patterns of love. We're all searching for familiarity.

6. I was *defining* relationships based on my parent's definition, not my own. Once I recognized that I had been living out someone else's definition of love, acting out motives that were not my own, and therefore making decisions based on someone else's patterns, I felt an immediate shift in my thinking.

7. I had no idea what a fulfilling relationship should look or feel like. So, I asked myself, "What is the foundation to all of my actions and decisions?" And the answer hit me hard; "I don't know." Up to that point in my life I had neglected to give any serious thought to what I actually wanted in and from a healthy relationship. I had a vague wish list of desired behaviors I wanted but on reflection I realized that none of those airy qualities actually supported my deepest belief system or Core Values.

8. The people and situations I attract are a direct result of what I believe about myself. I realized that my actions and decisions are guided by my belief system that includes my values (or beliefs, morals, virtues etc.).

9. Then I asked myself, "What are my Core Values, what do I believe?" Again I was surprised to realize that I didn't know. Based on my work experience, I knew that in successful companies, Corporate Values and Mission Statements increased decision-making skills, cohesiveness, as well as got people on 'the same page'.

10. I can attract relationships, friends and work experiences based on my own heart and spiritual insight. The relationships, people and situations you attract can only be fulfilling when matched with your own value system and then worked on, improved and exercised for greater experiences.

We all play an active role in our lives, which means that you alone are responsible for who and what you attract. The goal of **LLW** is to raise awareness of your Core Values so that you can knowingly move forward in life and attract fulfilling relationships, people and situations. The health factor of a relationship is then defined by how closely your reality matches your spiritual intention and not a characterization of any specific person or event.

Living and Loving Well enables you to reevaluate how you love, the choices you make and the people you allow in your life.

It will also help you appreciate the qualities that you do receive in your relationships, as well as identify those that need improving. The most wonderful thing about this field guide is that it will make you intensely aware of yourself. It will help you create your values, which again are the foundation to all of your future actions and decisions. It will also help you identify the relationships qualities you desire so that you can begin attracting more fulfilling relationships, or improve and fine-tune the relationships you already have.

It opens your mind to the possibility that love and relationships can be *what you want them to be*. It will both enable you to receive love and will give you the strength and know-how to wake up one day and be able to put more love back into the world.

I do not want to become unlike myself.

2

Love is a Pattern

According to many psychologists, our behavioral patterns, including how and whom we love, are developed by the age of six. As children our ability to communicate is minimal but the power to observe and mimic as a survival skill is deeply rooted in the genetic coding of our species. This means that the relationships we seek as adults imitate the dynamic we observed between our parents or caregivers (up to when we were 6). As we grew older and hopefully wiser, our parents may have tried to give contrary advice; "Do as I say, not as I do (or did)", but unfortunately the observed behavior was much more powerful than their contradicting advice.

Donna Wilshire, a friend of mine who writes about the Oral Tradition, explains that our species survived and thrived for many thousands of years without writing, without books. In the beginning, people communicated with each other and passed information down to the next generation through stories that were told orally, face-to-face, heavy with body language, and rooted in ritual and routine. Long before mankind could communicate through writing or, most recently, the Internet, humans learned through observation and repetition. This explains why the patterns we observed as children and that we now mimic seem to have more power over our behaviors than our intellects. In other words, we're smart enough to know better but find ourselves involved in situations (romance, friends or work) that go against our better judgment.

Survival skills are merely learned behaviors that determine how you'll respond to a given situation, but the word survival doesn't mean a healthy existence. Survival only means the continuation of life, or continuing to function.

Love is not only a pattern but it's also a future behavioral model that we 'default to' when we encounter similar situations. In other words, our caregivers acted as role models for our future relationships. The roles or dynamics that we observe become our 'emotional baseline' and act as templates that we apply to our relationships. The dynamic we observed in their relationships ultimately becomes the dynamic that we seek, especially since we mimic to survive. For example, if during the time between ages 0-6 the relationship you observed was full of criticism, the odds are very high that you will subconsciously seek criticism in your relationships even though you know that will not bring you happiness.

Drawing from my own experience, the relationship I observed up to the age of six involved unhealthy amounts of criticism. As I grew older I vowed to never allow criticism into my relationships but lo and behold, criticism was always strongly represented.

My default patterns dominated my behavior and reactions, which again, I learned through observation as a child. When a relationship presented itself, the deep-rooted pattern of criticism appeared and became a survival tactic that determined my reactions and behavior. Even though I was playing an active role in choosing a partner, my decisions and behaviors were determined by the highly critical patterns I observed in my parents.

On several occasions I told therapists that my patterns seemed greater than me, as if they had control over how I acted. Understanding why my patterns were so influential became the driving force for the creation and discovery of this **LLW** method. Patterns play a very powerful role in our lives. They have the ability to cloud our awareness of healthy human interaction because most of us are not taught how to exist in a healthy relationship, nor how to give love based on our own values and self-awareness. Our history limits us because we don't know what we don't know. Basic survival techniques in the animal world are taught to allow the next generation to endure and survive. Patterns that govern human emotion are no different regardless of their level of healthiness.

That also explains the common expression; "My husband [wife] was so different when we were dating. The minute we got married he [she] changed." People who appear to change like this may have only observed the husband/wife role, or survival skill in committed relationships. A dating role model may not have existed during their formative years. Therefore, so long as they were merely dating, they may have been able, at least somewhat, to define their own relationship roles and live together in a somewhat healthy relationship. As soon as the relationship became legal or committed, the default survival skills pop up and create a drastic change in personality. "He was fun while we were dating, but as soon as we got married he changed." Behaviors and reactions became consistent with what was learned and observed during those formative years.

Interestingly, it's also important to note that we can only attract those who have or seek the same dynamic – healthy or unhealthy. So, although the husband or wife is accused of drastically changing, they're both only capable of attracting what they know or observed. Most likely, they both had caretakers whose relationship exhibited a similar dynamic.

During my experience of teaching **LLW**, I've never come across anyone who attracted a dynamic different from his or her own. Those who spend the time defining love and establishing their personal values are those who move beyond their ingrained patterns and attract a dynamic closer to their heart. This concept is the foundation to **Living and Loving Well**. Once you define love and identify your own Core Values, the dynamic you seek and act out in life changes. The Universe provides what we actively acknowledge.

Observed roles are also gender neutral, which means that it doesn't matter which partner demonstrates the behavior, the familiar dynamic will be what you seek. This is proven in homosexual relationships since gender roles imposed by society over the years do not apply.

Over all, most individuals gravitate toward particular personality/character patterns when looking for a partner, which is why it's not uncommon to hear someone say, "She's just like her father" or "His mother was the same way". Familiarity is a strong reminder that we are a species that gravitates toward patterns.

Blame can also be mitigated when you acknowledge that your caregivers are caught up in the same pattern-driven cycle, their patterns were also established by the generation before them. Love and relationships are a generational pattern with slow progression.

Patterns can also be decidedly different between siblings, who can experience sharply contrasting dynamics based on the health of their caregiver's relationship during each sibling's formative years. A terrific example is of a young man who was very frustrated because he couldn't stay in a relationship longer than 5 weeks yet his sister (5 years older) had been happily married for 12 years. Upon a closer investigation, the young man discovered that his parents had been ecstatically happy for the first five years of their relationship, a terrific dynamic that the sister was fortunate to carry forward in her own life. By the time the son was born, the parent's relationship had soured. They lost their ability to communicate and eventually separated for one year, which became the foundation of the son's patterns. Same parents yet two children with opposing survival skills who attract completely different dynamics.

So it appears that we're all pattern junkies and unless educated otherwise, we'll default to a pattern, role, or dynamic that we learned via observation. At other times, given the right circumstances, we'll still go back to these default traits even though we know better. *This can often manifest as an inner conflict, or 'heart ache' because something 'doesn't feel right', which is simply you living a life based on generational patterns, and not according to your own spirit.*

We all have friends, family and acquaintances who repeat the same patterns over and over. Another example is of a young divorced mother, who raised her two children while experiencing a constant stream of unhealthy abusive relationships. When her children were toddlers they observed an unequal, desperate, disrespectful relationship.

As they grew, the children vowed that they 'wouldn't be caught dead' in a relationship like hers, which means that they must have known that it was wrong. The mother even advised her children: "don't do what I did, don't end up like me."

Sadly, when they were near the age of 18, both the son and daughter got involved in carbon copies of the abusive relationships they observed as children. The patterns and roles that had the strongest influence were fortified through observation and experience and not by oral advice and conversation.

As mentioned earlier, our species mimics to survive, which means the patterns we copy allow us to continue to function whether in a healthy mode or bad one. Often the survival skills we learn are dangerous and abusive, which is why **LLW** is so effective. It teaches one how to redefine relationships based on one's own intention and not someone else's destructive pattern or survival skill.

Historical Love

Throughout history, societies have made significant innovations in science, medicine and technology. Love, one of man's unique identifiers, is the only area that we have collectively not advanced. Love is all there is yet love remains the greatest mystery. Love's truest form escapes most of us because we were never taught effective skills for love, nor were we taught how to develop and honor our personal values, which act as the foundation for everything we attract in life. We think that love should come naturally but of course it doesn't. If you're like most, you've probably spent more time working on household chores than really thinking about love long enough to make ongoing positive change. We've been taught that power, fame and money, not love, are the key factors to a successful lifestyle.

Perfect love is usually communicated in movies and songs as forbidden, well timed, assumed, plagiarized, adulterous, completely effortless, last minute, homicidal, suicidal, incredibly desperate and always with THE ONE.

We've been raised on epic love stories like Antony and Cleopatra, or Romeo and Juliet, both of which end in double suicide, which in modern culture is usually the result of emotional instability, not to mention the fact that it's still against most legal and religious laws to kill yourself. Although very dramatic and intense, each is a poor example of the virtues of love. Epic love that we see in the media repeats a couple of different messages, the first being that our lives only have value if the other person exists to love us. Secondly, love is ALWAYS intensely passionate, destructive and/or borderline scary.

There are problems with these romantic images, the biggest being that they have nothing to do with the situations and people you bring into your life. Love should be a personal quest as defined by your own value system, not by a screenplay writer whom you've never met. 'Epic love' as portrayed in art, music, and literature creates internal conflict in all of us because it has the potential to contradict how we define love, as well as our own value system. We're spending time chasing someone else's version of love or the generational pattern that exists in our family.

Love Is Average

The basic scholastic bell curve also applies. The majority of what we learn about love falls into the average. Few people are actually taught the necessary skills to love, few are taught the extreme opposite, hate, and most of us fall into the center, having learned average skills in both love and hate. The bell curve shows us that love exists, and is taught as an average skill. If we only recognize an average understanding of love, we can only teach an average understanding of love. Our caregivers did not have the skills to teach us beyond their own average aptitude. On top of that, most of us haven't realized that the same rules do not apply to everyone. The value system that defines your mother or father, may not apply to you. Since love can only be defined by your own value system, it's up to you to define love as you see fit.

Imagine that we are 16th century explorers and our mission is to set sail for new lands. In our ship's hull we store gold, food and gifts that we will offer new peoples that we encounter. These gifts represent the best that our culture has to offer. By the time we arrive at our new destination we may only be able to offer merchandise that has been damaged during our voyage.

Now let's apply the same criteria to our present day adventure. When we first entered this world at birth, we arrived with only love. Love is the gold we brought with us as an offering to the new peoples we encounter. As other humans began interacting with us, perhaps our caregivers and neighbors, love took on a new shape based on our observations and experiences.

We adhere to the teachings of the people we 'trust' because we are not taught how to define love for ourselves. Before our first words are spoken our patterns of love have been established, and this is long before we are able to draw our own conclusions. We are then sent forth into the world with a damaged version of the merchandise we call love. Ironically, the etymology, or origin of the word 'average' from Old Italian *avaria* means damage to ship or cargo, and from Arabic *awArIyah*, means damaged merchandise. The love we offer those in our lives is oftentimes 'damaged merchandise' because it's been reshaped, twisted and manipulated from its original form. Our goal then is to discover the truth in ourselves so that we can redefine love according to our own spirit, which begins by identifying the values that govern our behaviors and decisions.

When love is absent, various levels of self-absorption fill the vacancy. If we are not taught how to love our ability to relate to others is drastically minimized which reduces our ability to establish healthy relationships based on our own intentions. Self-absorption is the opposite of being able to sustain a loving relationship, or the ability to attract positive people and situations.

Don't confuse self-absorption with pathology. Self-absorption is merely a lack of understanding of other people and their feelings, a lack of perspective about their opinions, values or even a lack of awareness of their presence. When we are not taught how to love, we are also not taught to be aware of others or that our actions have an affect on anyone else. We are not able to consciously incorporate into our thinking anything other than how the world affects us, our behavior, our feelings. Most of us recognize self-absorption in friends, family or parents, people whose behavior suggests a general disregard for the feelings or inclusion of others.

Of course there are varying degrees of self-absorption based on personal experiences. We all have different definitions of what love is but considering we're all part of the same species, true loving implies being aware of others, true love assumes generosity, compassion, and consideration for others.

3

Exploring Your Relationships

One of the goals of **LLW** is be to keep the process simple, which again means that the program is designed around the daily time constraints and heavy workloads of the modern day person. The pressure of everyday life does not allow most of us to take the time to discover who we are, which I believe results in our subconsciously working on autopilot especially when it comes to relationships. Think about it. We spend years educating ourselves on different disciplines but rarely do we spend time understanding other people, or how we want other people to love us. Typically we'll 'learn' something from a previous relationship and say, "I'll never do that again" but then find ourselves repeating the same pattern. The key to changing this is realizing that most of us haven't been taught how to align our Core Values with a personal definition of love. In other words, the Universe, God, Creation (or whom or whatever receives your prayers) only responds to the requests you make If you walk around the streets of your town with a vague understanding of love, then you can only be provided relationships that fulfill that hazy expectation and definition.

So off we go. Keep in mind that **LLW** is meant to offer one or two 'a-ha moments' that will become building blocks to bring healthier people and relationships into your life. BUT, just like everything else in the world, the results are up to you.

That said, below are the only four [4] written exercises that you will be asked to complete. You can either get a small journal for noting down observations about yourself and others, you can use the blank pages at the end of each chapter, or use any other method that suites your personal learning style.

1. Your Current Relationship Model
2. Create your Core Values
3. Create Life Statements
4. Your Improved Relationship Model w/ 'Ability Statements'

Throughout these exercises try to recall the dynamic and/or quality of the relationship between your parents, your caregivers, or if possible your grandparents, especially during those most formative years before you were six. You'll see that much of what you do in your current relationship was 'handed down' through the generations. A recurring theme in this guide is the expression, "You Don't Know What You Don't Know." We can take this one step farther and say that you can only teach what you know, so if you possess average skills for loving, then you can only teach average skills for loving. Note that the word 'teach' has an implied meaning that as children we learn via *observation and experience*.

Has anyone ever taken the time to teach you what it takes to maintain a healthy and fulfilling relationship? If so, how much time was spent doing it? How often have you evaluated the qualities of love that are of most value to you? In the last year, how much time have you spent evaluating the basic values that govern the relationships you bring into your life? On the other hand, how much time in that same year did you spend cleaning the bathroom, or washing dishes, ironing clothes or mowing the lawn?

Exercise 1

Your Current Relationship Model

Criteria & Guidelines

Step 1: Take a few minutes to write down the qualities that are important to have in your relationships. What do you look for in your relationships? Love, respect, or emotional safety? Remember that there are no right or wrong answers. If you need more room you can use the additional work sheet on page 19. Be true to yourself and your experiences. When you're finished continue to the second half of this exercise on the next page.

CURRENT RELATIONSHIP MODEL	
Ex 1 - Trust	
Ex 2 - Respect	

Step 2: Quantifying the exercise with eye-opening results!!

1. Using the qualities you just identified, let's see how they apply to your current and most recent relationship(s). They can include people that you're currently dating, or recent/past long-term relationships. Evaluate one relationship at a time.

2. Populate the gray column in the same table on page 16 with an accurate percentile of how often each quality existed in those relationships. Use the scale below to evaluate each:

Never	=	0
Rarely	=	.25
Sometimes	=	.50
Very Often	=	.75
Always	=	1.00

Please be very honest with this exercise.

3. Do this for the entire list of qualities. See example below.

	CURRENT RELATIONSHIP MODEL	
1	Trust	.50
2	Respect	.25
3	Fidelity	.50
4	Communication	.75
	Total	**2.00**

4. Add up the number of qualities in the <u>left</u> column. In the above there are 4 total qualities.

5. Add up the gray column on the right. In the above example the total comes to 2.00

6. Divide the right gray column by the left column which in the above example is 2.00/4 = 50%

7. In this example, the participant only receives 50% of the desirable qualities that are considered important to him/her. This shows that the participant can identify their important qualities but gets/seeks/attracts only 50%, proving that patterns play a powerful part in our relationships.

Some of you may be surprised that the number is lower than expected and some of you may have had a higher score than expected. Again, we attract people and situations based on generational patterns and not our internal definition of love and the basis to all of that are the values that govern all of our decisions.

Good job, you're one exercise closer to knowing more about yourself. Now, put the book away and go run your errands, and while you're at it, give some thought to what you wrote and give the 'This Is My Life' mantra (on page xx) a run through. Did the number of items you wrote surprise you? Were you expecting more or less? Do you feel that there may be more to your definition? Or do you think that this about sums it up?

This exercise is a good ongoing evaluation tool for any relationship in your life. If the percentile is low, it doesn't automatically indicate that the relationship must end, it's just identifies areas that you can improve on as a couple.

Additional Work Space

4

Defining Your Core Values

In this chapter we'll begin the process of understanding how values directly impact your decisions and actions. Whether you realize it or not, your life is guided by personal Core Values. We all have a subconscious list of values that steer us down different paths of life; unfortunately most of us aren't fully aware that they exist. Some may have been developed during difficult periods of our life, and others may have been part of the generational package we inherited from our caregivers. When not given the opportunity to create a set of governing values, you adopt many of your parent's behaviors and decision-making skills. Regardless of how they were established, they exist for all of us, yet very few of us can identify what they are. How can we make sound decisions (in any capacity of life) if we aren't aware of the values that direct our behaviors?

What is a Core Value?

Values are often described as ethics, virtues, beliefs, guiding principles, ideals and even a personal moral code for which to live life. Regardless of terminology they all share the same goal, which is to provide inner happiness, increased confidence, better decision-making, fulfilling relationships, create balance, clearer direction, and greater personal awareness. Core values act as rules or criteria for all of your decisions and actions. They guide our decision-making process and can range from how we choose our friends to our charitable actions or to the level of honor we exhibit in difficult situations. Our core values also cover various categories such as personal, social, aesthetic, religious, political, and health. They help us choose between good and bad, support and help establish our goals, give us a sense of purpose, and help us define work, friends, family and relationships.

Identifying your values is essential to understanding yourself and ultimately redefining your relationship qualities. *You'll then discover that love is not blind but a clear-guided effort based on your core belief system.*

For decades, successful corporations have also been using values, value statements, strategic planning, corporate vision and mission statements. They keep all layers in the organization aware of long and short-term goals, which let them communicate corporate ideologies. It also gives them direction and creates cohesiveness among the staff. To be a purpose driven individual we need to invest as much time and consideration into ourselves as successful corporation. Values can also focus and invigorate us by adding a sense of purpose, as well as make us better prepared to redefine how we look at love and relationships

Historically, values have long been recognized as an important factor to creating a happier, more fulfilling life. Great men from Aristotle to Benjamin Franklin wholeheartedly believed in the development of personal values. Thousands of years ago, the Greeks inscribed aphorisms, such as 'Know Thyself' and 'Nothing in Excess', in many spiritual locations. Aristotle adopted these same philosophies and created 7 virtues that he described as the 'mean' between good and bad excesses. At the age of 20, Benjamin Franklin, one of the most revered men in American history, crafted 13 values so that he could live a purpose driven life. These men lived thousands of years apart and in completely different times, yet shared the understanding that values helped them establish goals and achieve a positive and healthy way of living.

Benjamin Franklin believed in the following 13 values:

Temperance – Silence – Order – Resolution – Frugality – Industry – Sincerity – Justice – Moderation – Cleanliness – Tranquility – Chastity – Humility.

Aristotle named the following 7 virtues:

Courage – Temperance - Liberality – Magnificence – Pride – Gentleness -Agreeableness – Truthfulness – Wit

Exercise 2

Defining Your Core Values

The purpose of this exercise is to create your own set of Core Values that will act as criteria for all of your future actions and decisions. When you have completed this exercise, you'll not only have a greater understanding of yourself, you'll have a tool to guide you through the rest of your life.

Criteria & Guidelines

1. Break your life into categories such as health, spirituality, philanthropy, career, family, friends, creativity etc. These are main areas that encompass all of your life.

2. Using the categories you just created, go through the values list below and mark off all the values that speak to you and try to not to edit during this initial round. Be sure that all of your categories have been properly represented. You could possibly create a list up to 100 values.

3. Add any additional values that do not appear on the values list below. These could be items that you admire in other people.

4. Make a second and third pass if necessary through this new list and begin to eliminate and consolidate any repetitions or words that have similar meaning. For example, you may have separately checked off courage, fortitude, and determination, which all share similar definitions. Choose the value that best describes you.

5. Now it's time to make some decisions, your goal is to narrow it down to your top 10. It's not easy but you can do it. Review your list again and really choose the items that define YOU. Do not focus on negative images of yourself, or how you feel other people may perceive you. The purpose of this exercise is to create a set of values that guide your future actions and decision as defined by your ideal self.

It's o.k. to have 1 or 2 more but try to keep it as close as possible to a top 10. Remember that these should encompass all areas of your life. Eliminating values from your top 10 does not mean that they're not important to you.

Keep in mind that just because you're eliminating them from the core list, doesn't mean that they're not important. In a later exercise, we'll revisit the values that did not make your top 10.

a. For example, when I was writing my list, I really wanted to keep Beauty, not physical beauty rather the aesthetic beauty one sees in art. There's something about a beautiful sculpture that really moves me, BUT although I think it's important, it doesn't help guide my decisions in life, so I crossed it off my list of Core Values.

Here's what a sample list of values will look like. *Only use this as a reference*

1. Pride
2. Truthfulness
3. Charity
4. Health
5. Family/Friends
6. Communication
7. Balance
8. Cleanliness
9. Flexibility
10. Consistency

I encourage those of you that want to skip over this exercise to spend just a few minutes writing down the values that guide you through life. Change cannot occur without your participation. You don't have to commit half of your week; I'm only asking for one hour each week, so based on 168 hours in a week, it's less than 1% of your time.

Congratulations, you now have a list of top 10 values!! For three weeks, you should review the list every morning so that your subconscious can begin absorbing the new information. This is also an iterative process, which means that it would be helpful for you to review and update the list every 6-12 months. Your list should evolve with you through life.

LIST OF VALUES

Acceptance		Ethical Equality		Persistence	
Abundance		Excellence		Philanthropy	
Accomplishment		Experience		Piety	
Accountability		Expertise		Popularity	
Accuracy		Exploration		Positivism	
Achievement		Expressiveness		Potential	
Acknowledgement		Fairness		Power	
Activeness		Faith		Practicality	
Adaptability		Fame		Pragmatism	
Admiration		Family		Preparedness	
Adoration		Fearlessness		Preservation	
Adventure		Fidelity		Pride	
Affection		Fierceness		Privacy	
Affluence		Fitness		Proactive	
Agreeableness		Flexibility		Professionalism	
Altruism		Focus		Progress	
Ambition		Foresight		Prosperity	
Amiability		Forgiveness		Prudence	
Appreciation		Fortitude		Public Service	
Art		Free Will		Punctuality	
Assertiveness		Freedom		Purity	
Assurance		Friendliness		Purposefulness	
Attentiveness		Friendship		Quality	
Attractiveness		Frugality		Realism	
Autonomy		Fun		Reason	
Availability		Gallantry		Recognition	
Awareness		Generosity		Recreation	
Balance		Gentleness		Refinement	
Beauty		Giving		Reflection	
Belonging		Grace		Relaxation	
Benevolence		Gratitude		Reliability	
Bliss		Gregariousness		Religiousness	
Calmness		Growth		Resilience	
Caring		Guidance		Resolution	
Challenge		Happiness		Resourcefulness	
Change		Hard Work		Respectfulness	
Character		Harmony		Responsibility	
Charity		Health		Restraint	
Cleanliness		Heroism		Sacrifice	
Clear Mindedness		Holiness		Satisfaction	
Collaboration		Honesty		Security	
Comfort		Honor		Self Awareness	
Commitment		Hopefulness		Self Control	
Communication		Hospitality		Self Discipline	
Companionship		Humility		Self Esteem	
Compassion		Humor		Selflessness	
Competency		Hygiene		Self Motivation	
Completion		Idealism		Self Reliance	
Composure		Imagination		Self Respect	

LIST OF VALUES [continued]					
Compromise		Impartiality		Sensitivity	
Confidence		Improvement		Sensuality	
Conformity		Independence		Serenity	
Connection		Individuality		Service	
Consciousness		Industry		Sexuality	
Consideration		Influence		Sharing	
Consistency		Ingenuity		Shrewdness	
Contentment		Innocence		Significance	
Continuity		Innovativeness		Silence	
Control		Inspiration		Silliness	
Conviction		Integrity		Simplicity	
Cooperativeness		Intelligence		Sincerity	
Courage		Intensity		Skillfulness	
Courteousness		Intimacy		Solidarity	
Creativity		Intuition		Solitude	
Credibility		Inventiveness		Spirit	
Critical Thinking		Investing		Spirituality	
Cunning		Joyfulness		Spontaneity	
Curiosity		Judiciousness		Stability	
Daring		Justice		Stewardship	
Decisiveness		Kindness		Strength	
Dedication		Knowledge		Structure	
Dependability		Leadership		Success	
Depth		Learning		Support	
Desire		Liberty		Sympathy	
Detachment		Logic		Tactfulness	
Determination		Longevity		Teamwork	
Devotion		Lovingness		Temperance	
Dexterity		Loyalty		Thankfulness	
Dignity		Manners		Thoughtfulness	
Diligence		Maturity		Thrift	
Direction		Mercy		Tolerance	
Discovery		Modesty		Tranquility	
Diversity		Money		Transcendence	
Duty		Morality		Trust	
Eagerness		Motivation		Truth	
Ecstasy		Nonviolence		Understanding	
Education		Nurturing		Uniqueness	
Effectiveness		Obedience		Unity	
Efficiency		Open Mindedness		Unselfishness	
Effort		Optimism		Usefulness	
Empathy		Order		Utility	
Empowerment		Organization		Valor	
Encouragement		Originality		Vision	
Endurance		Patience		Vitality	
Energy		Patriotism		Wealth	
Enjoyment		Peace		Willingness	
Entertainment		Peacefulness		Wisdom	
Equality		Perseverance		Wit	

Additional Work Space

5

Creating your 'Life Statements'

The majority of individuals I speak with react to circumstance as if the status quo is the only option. It's not unusual to hear someone say, "Well, what else am I going to do?" to which I always respond, "Have you thought about your options?" This is all part of the larger cycle that nurtures our unhealthy patterns. From the beginning, our survival mechanism grabs hold of a default role that we subconsciously follow. It's easy to assume that the role we play is limited and without alternative options, because we easily gravitate toward what is known which means that our sub-conscious blocks our ability to see different solutions. It's a strange malady that we oftentimes only have the ability to recognize what is known. To make the situation more complicated, many of us are afraid of the unknown, we're fearful of what we do not know, so we accept the comfort of living against our internal beliefs in the world around us, instead of realizing that we all have options. Sadly, we sometimes aren't aware that they exist.

For those reasons, it's important to do a little soul searching so that you can add Life Statements to your newly established Values. The purpose is not to change who you are, but to extract information about your core self. You only need to clarify and refocus your belief system so that the Universe can respond to your clear intentions. With that said, our goal for much of this process is to recognize your true self that has existed since birth.

Exercise 3

Creating Your Life Statements

Now that you've unearthed your Core Values in the previous exercise, let's build off of them and create supporting "Life Statements", which is the third step in this process. These statements are similar to Mission Statements subscribed to by large and small corporations around the globe. Remember, your values create a set of defining beliefs that act as the foundation to your self. *Life Statements embrace your Core Values in addition to other beliefs and tenets, and then distribute them among all categories of your life.*

Think of your spirit as an internal CEO, who guides you through life. If the CEO doesn't offer the company a mission statement or future vision, his employees move about chaotically without direction or focus. Most of us spend our days in similar confusion, because we haven't defined our values and life statements. The following is a terrific example of a corporate Mission Statement by Ben & Jerry's Ice Cream.

"To make, distribute & sell the finest quality all natural ice cream & euphoric concoctions with a continued commitment to incorporating wholesome, natural ingredients and promoting business practices that respect the Earth and the Environment."

Every employee can deduce from this statement the company values: using natural ingredients, creativity, eco-friendly practices and making money. It's very simple and to the point but still packs a punch. If they ever had to make a decision about whether to recycle or to use landfills, they would most likely opt to recycle, unless of course, they don't stand behind their values.

Let's review a possible set of Core Values from the previous chapter. These will be one-word beliefs that support your personal code of conduct. They could be:

- Health
- Balance
- Honor

Life Statements are 1 or 2 specific sentences that support your life categories AND your values. This is where you can incorporate some of the values that did not make it to your top ten Core Values list. Life Statements are like personal mantras developed by you, according to your will.

Life Statements can be created using some of the various styles shown below.

Using the "I VALUE" statement

Example 1:
I VALUE a healthy lifestyle. I place great importance on proper diet and exercise as a means to live a disease-free and more energy influenced life.

Example 2:
I VALUE a strong balance between work, play and relaxation. I will not compromise my personal growth, and recognize that my actions have an outward effect on the people and world around me.

[Note: These examples incorporate various life categories and values]

Using the "I WILL" statement

Example 1:
I WILL live a healthy lifestyle. I place great importance on proper diet and exercise as a means to live a disease-free and more energy influenced life.

Example 2:
I WILL balance work, play and relaxation. I will not compromise my personal growth, and recognize that my actions have an outward effect on the people and world around me

Using General Statements

Example 1:
For as long as I can, I will keep my mind, body and spirit strong, so that I can experience this sweet life to its fullest.

Example 2:
To thine own self be true

Example 3:
By honoring my values, I honor myself
(I recommend that this be on everyone's list)

Example 4:
My life incorporates a balanced approach to work, play and relaxation. I do not compromise my personal growth, and recognize that my actions have an outward effect on the people and world around me.

Note again that these statements reflect more than one category; work, play, relaxation, personal growth, consideration and compassion. The last example also incorporates 3 different elements of one's life: mental, physical and spiritual health

Criteria and Guidelines:

- Keep them POSITIVE. Do not use negative comments such as 'I will not eat cheese…'. Flip it into a positive intention such as 'I will eat nutritiously to…'.
- Keep statements simple and to the point. 1 or 2 sentences for each.
- Life Statements can have various styles;
  - o   I value…..
  - o   I will……..
  - o   Or general statements
- Make sure to incorporate ALL of your Core Values. This does not mean that all Life Statements need to contain every value. In other words, if you have 10 Core Values then a Life Statement may support 1 or more Core Values.
- Incorporate additional beliefs and tenets that 'speak to you'.
- Life Statements should span all of *your* life categories, which vary by person. A category can be covered in one or more Life Statements.
- Keep the number of Life Statements limited to 10 or 15
- Eliminate repetition. Core Values should only appear in one Life Statement. So for example, you shouldn't have a statement that uses charity and another that uses philanthropy. They should be incorporated into the same statement or consolidated into one.
- Incorporate your negative behaviors or patterns as a means to grow. For example, if you know that you act with intolerance be sure to say, "I will act with tolerance so that I may set an example for my children."

Here's a sample list of Life Statements

1. By honoring my values, I honor myself.

2. For as long as I can, I will keep my mind, body and spirit strong, so that I can experience this sweet life to its fullest.

3. I believe in ultimate justice.

4. I respect the potency of money, compassion and charity, and I will use each to make a positive impact on the world.

5. I trust the Universe to guide my actions, so that my faith may protect my spirit.

6. I will balance work, play and relaxation. I will not compromise my personal growth. I will recognize that my actions have an effect on the people and world around me.

7. I will build supportive, loyal and committed relationships. I will act with tolerance, humor, understanding, truth and open mindedness and I will treat others, as I would like to be treated.

8. I will recognize those who helped me along the way and show them my gratitude

Now have some fun and create your Life Statements.

Please use the Statements above as a guide ONLY. The idea is to define your Life Statements based on your own spirit, not a random sampling found on this page.

	YOUR LIFE STATEMENTS
1	
2	
3	
4	
5	
6	
7	
8	
9	
10	
11	
12	
13	
14	
15	

Additional Work Space

6

Living and Loving Well

You are now going to create your Improved Relationship Model. By now I hope you can see that the work you've done to create your values and Life Statement(s) acts as a strong foundation for this last exercise.

Let me reiterate three very important points:

1. Love encompasses all aspects and all people in our lives so when I mention relationships and love, I'm talking about ALL relationships including; family, friends, work and romance. Our marital and loving relationships are not the only dynamics that can demonstrate old patterns. Of course, you must exercise flexibility since items such as monogamy will only apply to romantic relationships and not to work situations.

2. All of the qualities listed in your final definition must be mutually reciprocated. This means that you are as responsible for exhibiting the behavior, as you are to desire it. You cannot ask for something unless you are willing to provide the same.

3. All relationships have a cause and effect association. In other words, your actions, behaviors, responses, expressions and desires have a ripple effect in the world around you.

It's time to erase all the old ideals and expectations that you have of love. Eliminate the media driven fallacies and the romanticized dramas that have followed us through history. As I mentioned earlier, love is a personal experience that should support your values and beliefs. If you believe that what you've done here is truthful and relevant, then you are responsible for acting accordingly.

** The key for this entire effort to be successful is that you must believe in the words you've written. Sometimes it's more powerful to believe something will happen than understanding how it will occur! **

Once you do all this work you may find yourself being tested by God, Creation, the Universe or by the situations and people around you. These tests are simply your old patterns and definitions trying to rear their ugly heads.

Getting yourself to live and breath your newly realized self, will be like exercising any other muscle in your body. It takes work and commitment to achieve your end result, but the great thing about it is that you now know where you're going. We've paved a clear roadway with your values and beliefs.

For example, if you've discovered through this process of evaluation that you value Gratitude as a core belief, you'll be more aware of how others display thankfulness, as well as how you respond to the charity of others. You've opened your eyes to your own spirit, so the world around you is merely waiting for your lead.

Exercise 4

The Improved Relationship Model

The purpose of the Relationship Model is to create a specific list of qualities and intentions for you to attract in life, and that are based on your Core Values. For example, in Exercise 1 you listed 10 qualities you found important in your relationships. But it may turn out that you only attracted 40% of those qualities. With your values and Life Statements defined, you can create a list of the relationships qualities that you desire, so that the Universe can respond to your clear and focused intentions, as opposed to a hazy idea of what you desire.

Update the Relationship Model – Step by Step
Spend some time consolidating the relationship qualities you now want to attract for all of the relationships in your life.

Step 1: Consolidating all your qualities
Use the blank sheets at the end of the chapter to complete this exercise.

    a.   Write down *all* of your Core Values
    b.   Write down *all* of the other values that did not make it to your top ten. So if you originally marked off 50 values, and then ended up with 10 Core Values, you should be able to add 40 additional items to this list.
    c.   Include *all* of the original qualities from the first Relationship Model you completed in the first exercise on page 16.
    d.   Include any qualities that you admire in other couples.
    e.   Add the opposite of any negative qualities you identified. Fore example, instead of putting "lying" on the list, be sure "truthfulness" exists.
    f.   Eliminate duplicates.
    g.   When you feel you have a full list of qualities, it's time to narrow things down. Just as with your list of values, your first pass may have generated a many items. This list can easily include over 100 qualities.

h. Step away from the list for a bit. Go shopping or have a cup of tea, and then come back and strip it down to the essentials, down to the core fundamentals that you want to exist in your relationships. Do this a couple times until you have eliminated the peripheral items. This step will be a challenge but stick with it.

i. Don't set yourself up for failure. I recommend that you keep your final list under 35 items, otherwise you're time is spent managing a list rather than attracting healthy situations. Of course, this is flexible based on your needs.

j. Remember to consolidate repetitive items when possible.

k. **Transfer your final consolidated list of qualities [under 35 items] into the 'Qualities' column of the 'Improved Relationship Model' on page 43-44**

This list of qualities is the first step to improving your Relationship Model, only one more step to go. In the beginning, it's very likely that you weren't fully cognizant of the items in this final list at all, or they may have been in the back of your mind. Bringing them to the surface allows the Universe to respond to them as clear and focused intentions.

Remember, the purpose of this entire process is to heighten awareness of your spiritual intentions by re-defining what you want. Many of our behaviors, actions and reactions are governed by patterns we inherit from the previous generation. These patterns can oftentimes oppose our core self, which create internal conflict that is exceedingly difficult to resolve simply because we're not aware the conflict exists. Clearly defining your values, life statements and relationship model eliminates much of that conflict because you attract situation and people based on spiritual clarity.

Additional Work Space

Step 2: –Adding Your Ability Statements

Ok, this is the last part required to finalize your Improved Relationship Model. You've come a long way, so please give yourself kudos for getting this far. You're going to create 'Ability Statements' around each positive quality that you've chosen for yourself. These are the (35 or less) qualities.

'Ability Statements' are personal and specific declarations about your own spirit. They should not be generic statements because you are not generic. You are a unique individual among more than 6 billion people in the world. These 'Ability Statements' give intention to your positive qualities. Many times people will list trust as important in a relationship but trust has many meanings so be specific. Does it mean you provide emotional safety to one another? Or that fidelity is important to both you and your partner? Or that each of you has the ability to share secrets? Or does it mean all three? You're the only one who can identify the meaning so it's important to define each quality so that the Universe can respond with specificity rather than vagueness.

Here are examples of 'Ability Statements':

Commitment	The ability to pledge a commitment to another without fear or apprehension.
Empathy	The ability to understand and support the humility, pain, discomfort or sorrow of another.
Equality	The ability to maintain a respectful level of equality in all areas of the relationship including opinions, goals, desires and responsibilities.
Playfulness	The ability to be silly together.
Trust	The ability to live without fear of negative repercussions as well as live monogamously.

Criteria & Guidelines:

1. Keep it simple and succinct. Only 1-2 sentences per quality.
2. Do not edit your thoughts. Allow yourself to be truthful to the meaning of each quality.
3. Relationships are comprised of two people so share the responsibility. Each statement holds mutual responsibility in every relationship.
4. They should all begin with the words 'The ability'. In your mind begin each statement by saying 'In my relationships, each of us has the ability to.......'. This may help you understand the meaning. In other words, if I use the example of Playfulness from above, I could say, 'In my relationships, each of us has the ability to be silly together.'
5. Walk away for a bit, then review the list with a clear head. Do they still make sense? If not, make any necessary changes.

IMPROVED RELATIONSHIP MODEL	
Qualities	**'Ability Statements'**
i.e. Commitment	*i.e. The ability to pledge a commitment to another without fear or apprehension.*
	The ability to
	The ability to
	The ability to
	The ability to
	The ability to
	The ability to
	The ability to
	The ability to
	The ability to
	The ability to
	The ability to
	The ability to
	The ability to
	The ability to
	The ability to
	The ability to
	The ability to
	The ability to

IMPROVED RELATIONSHIP MODEL	
Qualities	**'Ability Statements'**
i.e. Commitment	*i.e. The ability to pledge a commitment to another without fear or apprehension.*
	The ability to
	The ability to
	The ability to
	The ability to
	The ability to
	The ability to
	The ability to
	The ability to
	The ability to
	The ability to
	The ability to
	The ability to
	The ability to
	The ability to
	The ability to
	The ability to
	The ability to
	The ability to
	The ability to

Congratulations!! You're done.

The last thing to do it to print out a clean copy of your Core Values, your Life Statements and your Improved Relationship Model, and keep them somewhere that can be accessed daily. I recommend that for the first few weeks, you read all three out loud to yourself so that your subconscious gets the chance to really absorb the information.

*** Remember that this is an iterative process. As you change through life, your Values, Life Statements and Relationship Model may change too. It's recommended that you refine your list every year or two, or whenever you feel it's necessary. It may stay the same or you may only have to make slight changes. These are great tools to use for helping yourself evaluate situations and relationships. ***

Great job! You've gone from living life based on someone's else's definitions and patterns to living and loving well based on your own spirit and desire.

If you have any questions, please feel free to contact us at:

info@livingandlovingwell.com

Additional Work Space

Additional Work Space

Additional Work Space

Additional Work Space

CPSIA information can be obtained at www.ICGtesting.com
Printed in the USA
LVOW13s0308270114

371096LV00001B/376/P